HOW TO WRITE A NOVELLA IN 24 HOURS

This printed book was adapted from the ebook version. Some of my delightful jokes attempting to get you to click on a link to sign up for my email list probably won't work so well on paper. So just go to AndrewMayne.com and join there.

Special thanks to my parents.

TABLE OF CONTENTS

HOW TO WRITE A NOVELLA IN 24 HOURS

AND OTHER QUESTIONABLE & POSSIBLY INSANE ADVICE ON CREATIVITY FOR WRITERS

ANDREW MAYNE

INTRODUCTION

This slim volume is a collection of some of the things I've learned as a writer trying to understand our craft a little more.

The title, **How to write a fiction book in 24 Hours**, is a practical how to guide and not some gimmicky promise with a lot of caveats. In a little over 2,000 words, I explain the seven most important points I learned in my little experiment that's now become a regular habit of mine. I think marathon writing (a real writing marathon – not NaNoWriMo 30-day writing) is great training for a writer. What you produce doesn't have to be released to the unsuspecting public. Finishing anything in this period, a novella, a novelette or a short story, shows that you're capable of finishing things. Finishing things is the key to much in life.

Before I wrote my first novel, *Public Enemy Zero*, writing a full-length novel seemed like an impossible ordeal. I cut my teeth with a 30,000-word novella, *The Grendel's*

Shadow, and realized it was just a matter of passion, patience and idea. If you have all three, you're going to do fine.

My goal with this collection of essays is to help you get through those times when one or more of them is suffering.

How to start building your empire is about starting the growth of your audience and how to guarantee that when you have something to say, there will be someone to listen.

How long should a story be? Answers a very basic question similar to the one aspiring filmmakers ask when they wonder, where should they point the camera? (Check out David Mamet's book *On Directing Film* for the answer to that.)

How to write a bestselling novel on your iPhone, is my productivity secret. If you can master this, you'll thank me profusely. I was determined to be able to write anywhere, anytime and doing so has enabled me to write in casinos, airplanes and in the bathroom more than we need to talk about.

In **The secret to making a book cover (that mostly doesn't suck) in 10 minutes or less,** I show the very simple formula behind most of the iconic book covers of all time and how to use it to make your own cover in ten minutes (and then explain why you should make a bunch of them and refine the one you like the most.)

With **Why you're staring at a blank screen**, I try to break down writer's block and the reason beginning writers find themselves trying to figure out what to write instead of actually writing.

One Weird Trick to Boost Your Creativity, is a very simple thing you can do to build a war chest of countless ideas.

In **Your worst idea may be your greatest**, I explain how one of the greatest storytelling franchises of all time was almost a disaster and try to show you how great things come in iterations, not all at once.

You suck at taking criticism explains how a relentless pursuit of improvement is the key to success. Rather than "ignoring" negative people or criticism, great artists find a way to understand and learn from it.

In **The Curse of a Creative Mind**, I'll tell you how to figure out which idea of yours is the best one and explain why you can't get anything done.

How to Make Sure Your Self-Published Book Doesn't Look Self-Published, is ten pieces of advice on how to avoid common self-publishing mistakes when you print your book. (Spoiler: Don't say "By" before your name on the cover.

What are my favorite tools for writing books? Oddly enough, I explain in **My 5 Favorite Writing Tools**.

I discuss the trick question of titling your book in **How I named this book**.

Finally, **100 No (or low) Cost Ways to Promote Your Ebook**, is a list of ideas meant to jumpstart your promotion of your books.

I hope you find something useful here!

Best,

Andrew Mayne
@AndrewMayne

HOW TO WRITE A NOVELLA IN 24 HOURS

What is this madness?

First off, let's discuss what I mean by a book. I'm not talking about writing the next *Game of Thrones* opus. Although it would be wonderful if GRR could pick up the pace just a little bit...

When I say "book" I mean a novella. What's a novella? According to the Science Fiction and Fantasy Writers of America, a novella is anything from 17,500 words to 40,000. Whereas a novel is anything over 40,000. What kind of books fall under the novella category? Lemony Snicket's *A Series of Unfortunate Events*, George Orwell's *Animal Farm*, all of R.L. Stine's *Goosebumps* books, lots of Stephen King stories, including *Rita Hayworth and the Shawshank Redemption* – IMDB's best rated movie of all time, *Shawshank Redemption*, is based on. Richard Matheson's *I Am Legend*, and so on.

My point is there are lots of great books that fall under the category of "novella." And quite a few have made great movies. There would probably be a great deal more if the logistics of publishing were friendlier towards that medium. But guess what? In the age of the Kindle, those rules don't apply. There's been a renaissance of the novella thanks to ebooks.

What's also great about this size is that for a dedicated human being, you can write something like this in one or two sittings. As an experiment, fresh off finishing a novel, I was eager to write a shorter book and committed myself to writing a novella in 24 hours.

Why this madness?

I decided to try writing a novella in 24 hours because I was afraid I was becoming complacent in my writing. My first year of writing (and making money doing it) I wrote something like 8 or 10 books. Since then I got a little lazy. Granted, I did things like make a television show, but still, I watched myself take longer and longer to write and develop some bad habits.

After taking an egregiously long time to finish one book (3 months – which is an eternity for me), I sat down and made note of all the things that went wrong. The book I wrote after that came together in a fun two weeks of writing that never felt forced.

Right after I finished, I made note of everything that worked and how I was in the "zone." This all took place at an In-N-Out Burger where I was celebrating the completion of the novel. While sitting there I had an idea for a cool story and put it aside for a moment. I was focused on my average word count and realized that it was about 4,000 a day on the novel. Some days I did 10,000, but mostly it was around 2,000 to 4,000 words.

While eating my animal-style fries I remembered how during my first year of writing I once did 17,000 words in one day – words that ended up in my book *The Chronological Man: The Monster in the Mist*, a series that I get just as many people pestering me for more sequels as anything else I've ever done (Including Jessica Blackwood books).

Could I write that many words in a day again or was that just a fleeting experience that happened out of boredom and desperation?

I suddenly realized that the story in the back of my head (a kind of horror adventure) would make a perfect novella – one that I could wrap up in 17,500 words (or so.)

I went home, and instead of lounging around for a few days patting myself on the back for finishing the other book, I made a little one-page outline and went to work. I wrote from 5 pm to about 3 AM – passing my 17,000 earlier record that evening when I counted what I'd done in the last 24 hours on the other book. I went to sleep and then got back up around 8:30 AM and jumped back behind the keyboard.

I finished at 4:45 PM, less than 24 hours later, with a word count of 20,053. I'd written an entire novella – an honest to goodness book in less than a day.

For me it was like completing a marathon and not dying on the finish line. It felt great. Not only had I broken my previous record, I actually got a little sleep and wrote something roughly coherent.

Is it any good?
It's a mess – just like all my other first drafts. I probably have thousand of confused homonyms and other typical mistakes. It'll take some loving attention before I let

anyone else read it. But for me, the hard part is done. The story is there. Editing and revising will be fun.

Other than my rampant typos, I love how the story turned out. Writing at the pace I did, kept the action moving and made for something I think has theatrical potential.

As I mentioned before, the last time I wrote at this pace, I typed half a book people still tell me is one of their favorites. And I understand why; as I wrote it I was with my characters Smith and April every step of the way. It was a magical experience where I felt like I was really there. That happened with this novella too. I can't wait to share it. But anyway...

How do you do this sorcery?
I'm going to let you in on a secret. You're going to look at this screen and say to yourself, "Andrew is an idiot. That's the most obvious thing in the world," and you'd be right. But moving right past that, in the five years I've been writing and making money from books sales, TV and films deals, blackmail plots, etc., I didn't realize something until a few weeks ago. Get ready to call me an idiot...
I write the fastest when I already know what the hell I'm writing about. I don't mean the plot – I always have part of that figured out. What I mean is that if I'm making up something in my head using places and situations I already know, then it goes smoothly. If on the other hand, I'm writing about Norway or the Eemian interglacial period, then I'm going to be jumping in and out of the story checking facts and making sure I don't embarrass myself too much.

Write what you know(ish)

They say "Write what you know." It's generally good advice but needs a lot of qualifiers. You're allowed to write about anything: Ancient Rome, far off alien civilizations, the opposite sex, it's all fair game. The key is to play to your strengths. Don't be afraid to expand them either. But when you want to write something really, really fast, stick to all the stuff in your head.

Pick the right kind of story

A novella generally focuses on one character or storyline. Fun fact: Most of the big huge epic tomes you read (*Game of Thrones*, etc,) are actually a bunch of novellas tied together. Think about big books where the story jumps from different groups of characters. They all have their plots tied up in that bigger one, and they may end up together, but the book is really collection of stories from different points of view.

When you write your novella you need a story that can be told in under 40,000 words. The more characters and side plots, the thinner the telling is going to be. Don't choose this format because you're too lazy to tell your sprawling epic they way it should be done. Choose it because you have a tight story that is best served by this format.

I highly recommend you go read the books I mentioned earlier for examples:

I Am Legend
Animal Farm
Rita Hayworth and the Shawshank Redemption
Lemony Snicket's A Series of Unfortunate Events

Character, character, character

Know your characters when you sit down. People often write character descriptions like the back of a baseball card. How someone will handle a situation is more important than the city of their birth and if they have dirty blonde or straw-colored hair – have that information too, but write about a soul, not a body.

Create your zone

Besides wearing comfy clothes, I write with noise-canceling earbuds. They're the small in-ear kind. Lately, I don't even listen to music. I just use them to tune out the world – which probably means I'm a sociopath. My phone is face down on the couch and I don't have any pop-up notifications on my computer.

If you're in a jam because gunmen have invaded your Costa Rican hotel and are going room-to-room robbing people, don't bother calling me. I'm in the zone. This actually happened to my best friend, Ken. He called. I didn't pick up. Sorry man. It turned out fine, FYI. Nobody got killed and I got to write. Win Win.

Outline - but not too much

I've gone through phases where I make super-detailed outlines starting with legal pads, sketching out scenes, filling out note cards and then redoing everything. For my novella I limited myself to just a bare bones outline of literally seven or eight bullet points and a couple pages of notes. I wrote down the beats I wanted to hit, but otherwise let my imagination run wild when I wrote. It was a great experience that gave me enough structure to know where to start and end, but the freedom to change things up as I saw fit.

Have a solid ending in mind

Some writers like to leave things open ended and try to meander towards a conclusion. I think when you're writing something like a novella in 24 hours, it's a good idea to have a very specific end point in mind. This doesn't mean you can't go in a different direction when you get there, but having a resolution will really help you focus on the story.

Just write the damn thing!

In the end it doesn't matter if you write the book in 24 hours, 24 days or 24 years. The thing that is important is that you enjoy (most of the time) the process of taking those tortured little sparks of imagination in your head and giving them concrete form in the this world.

Don't judge yourself by other people's productivity. The more you write, the better you'll understand what's right for you. I've released more books than J.K. Rowling, but last I checked, the lady is managing just fine. Everyone's mileage will vary, what matters is that you enjoy the trip. Also, avoid metaphors.

So...why not write a real novel in 24 hours?

I write about 1,500 to 2,000 words an hour comfortably. By "write", I mean create. Some people confuse writing speed with typing speed. One is creative, the other is just letting something pass through your eyes or ears without processing. You'll sometimes hear about a famous author that could write a zillion words a minute. So can a court reporter. The critical question is how much they can create.

The fastest authors I know of (like Isaac Asimov – who reportedly would talk on the phone and type at the same time) tend to write at the speed of a fast talker.

To produce a novel (40,000 words) in a day would mean writing 1,700 words an hour. That's within my range, but not after being up for 24 hours straight. I tried a 5 hour energy drink during my 24 hour binge. I was literally dancing twenty minutes after I downed it. An hour later I crashed. The next day I was jittery as hell.

That being said, at some point I'll try this when I have a good idea of how to manage my need for rest. I make no promises to quality. I read a couple of examples of novels written in 24 hours by some other mad men. Besides the inevitably grammatical mistakes, they were horrible. Trying to read them made my head hurt and question the entire premise of writing so much in one period.

If I hadn't had the prior experience of publishing something quickly written that was well-received, I'd have dismissed the whole concept as a fool's errand. But that being said, I don't know if it's possible to write a good novel in 24 hours. Right now I'm happy with novellas. It's fun to do and I get to sleep.

Summing it all up, here are the seven steps to writing a book in 24 hours:

1. Choose a story based on locations and events you're already familiar with.

2. Pick a story that is a suitable length for a novella.

3. Write down a solid character description before you start and understand how they'd try to deal with the conflict you present them.

4. Get comfortable and settle in for the long haul.

5. Outline your story enough that you have a map, but not too much that you feel like you're just filling in a tax form.

6. Have a destination in mind; know when the conflict will be over.

7. Don't overthink it. Just write.

How to start building your empire

Money is nice. Power is better. And its less psychotic cousin, influence, is pretty cool too.

One of the most shocking revelations for celebrities accustomed to the old media world is how little people care about what they have to say when it doesn't pertain to their work or involving something outrageous.

A certain pair of celebrity sisters whose reality television career was launched when their older sister's sex tape was "accidentally" leaked, put out a dystopian YA novel last year to a great amount of fanfare (ghost written, of course). Publishers thought they had a sure-fire hit. Their combined Instagram accounts numbered in the gazillions and they were about as super-famous as you could get. The girls did tons of press and talked about the book everywhere.

The book was considered a bomb. For all the hype, it barely moved the needle and got horrible reviews. What was hoped to be a start of a huge franchise encompassing books, films and everything in between, was just one other example of a highly promoted celebrity book that tanked.

If people who grace the covers of magazines every month can fail, then what chance do us less artificially enhanced photogenic mortals have?

Statistically, the odds are against us. First there's the fact that 99% of self-released books just aren't very good. The second fact, that even if it's good, it can be real hard to get anyone to notice.

That's why you need to increase your odds of getting attention. And that starts by building up your audience – your "Empire": The number of people you can reach out to. I don't mean some imaginary group of people out there you think are kind of fond of you, I mean an actual quantifiable number of people that you have direct contact with.

It's also important to keep in mind that not everyone who likes you will like your stuff. My mother has probably only read two of my books. My closest friends have suspiciously dusty copies of my books on their shelves they "can't wait to read." Likewise, I like lots of people, but their thing isn't my thing. I have close to 300,000 Twitter followers. Most of them like me as the guy that pulls magic pranks on people.

I like social media, but my real empire is my mailing list. This a group of self-selected people who have said, "Yes, Andrew, please tell me what you're doing next."

Unlike Facebook, where you have to pay for your posts to get seen, or Twitter, where you pray that people are watching your feed when you tweet something vital out, an email list is the most surefire way to make sure your message at least has a chance of reaching the people you want to see it.

Email lists are crucial for authors and anyone else who wants to promote something. They also take time to build.

I know a few people whose careers have suffered because they never got a list started and suddenly found themselves with a very tiny megaphone and nobody to point it to.

Don't let this happen to you. Build an email list. Start now. Like, right now. You can begin by just saving email addresses and then moving onto a paid service. A tiny list, even a few dozen people you know, can be wonderful. Those are the first people to hear about your book and the first ones to review it. Even one person can make a difference.

There are lots of great resources that go into detail on this, but here are my pointers on how anyone can start a list:

1. Email everyone in your contact list and ask them if they'd like to be on your email list. If they make the choice to be on the list they'll be more invested in it.

2. Create a link to your list signup on your web page (Yes, you need a web page) and change your signature line on your email to include a signup link for your list.

3. Send out regular reminders on your social media (even if you have ten followers).

4. Put a link to your email list in your ebooks.

5. Ask one of your friends if you can cross-promote your list with theirs. Keep asking...

6. Mention your email list in every club or activity you're involved with. Physically hand people your phone with a signup form.

7. Join groups and go to activities where you'll meet prospective list joiners (book clubs, writing groups, etc.)

8. Offer free books to people who retweet your signup link. Consider offering marriage proposals.

9. Put. Your. Signup. Link. Everywhere.

10. Give people a reason to signup. (Did I mention I like to send free ebooks to people who sign up for my email list?)

How long should a story be?

You have a great idea and you want to turn it into a story. Should it be a short? A novella? A novel? Or an entire series?

The answer to this isn't quite simple, but there's a couple ways to look at it that can help you figure out what would be best.

How many things are taking place?
In an epic series like G.R.R. Martin's *Song of Ice and Fire* saga (*Game of Thrones* to television watchers) we're watching hundreds of characters interact as the fate of civilization hangs in the balance. Obviously this is heady stuff and can't happen in a few dozen (or thousand pages). There's no way to tell the story on a human-scale and not making it a sprawling tale of several books.

Is there a big character arc?
A story doesn't have to involve queens and kingdoms to fill a thick novel. If you're telling the account of a person going through a life-changing event where they come out altered on the other side, showing their journey might involve a lot of slice-of-life scenes that require you to move at a pace that feels like real-time to readers. They don't just grab dinner and a movie with a date. They watch the other over the menu, try to guess what they're going to choose, notice the couple at the table in the corner arguing over their child's table manners, etc. The more specific the details, the more real it will feel. If all those little observations play into your character's state of mind and have the potential to change things, then they're important. If not, then it probably won't be that interesting.

Is the premise more important than the characters?
A joke is a story. It has a beginning, a middle and a (hopefully) surprise ending. Like short stories, they often deal in archetypes or people the reader can relate to. The point of a joke or a short story is usually to convey one single theme. O. Henry stories were usually small pithy tales of irony. Edgar Allan Poe's stories often pulled you into a dark corner of someone's psyche. His central character is often the reader, such as in The Tell-Tale Heart where the narrator is trying to convince us that he's quite sane, when in fact revealing he's anything but. Murder mystery shorts are usually about an event; a detective is a quirky archetype, as are all the other characters. Our interest in those kinds of stories is how it happened, not so much the character arc and reasons why.

A novel or a novella?

There aren't any hard and fast rules to the difference between these. Some great books, like Animal Farm are quite short (30,000 words). Other novels, often fantasy, can be ten times that size. Often a novel is comprised of what can be described as several novellas about different characters. If a story jumps from person to person between chapters and they have different goals for most of it, their own story might break down into something novella-sized or shorter.

Take a look at how many characters you have and the size of the conflict. This can tell you what length you should shoot for. If you think your idea is too big for a short or novella, then ask yourself how that event affects other people. Is their story worth telling too? The movie *Apollo 13* featured the plight of astronauts in a broken spacecraft, but much of the drama happened on earth as we watched Mission Control try to come up with solutions and their loved ones cope with the potential tragedy. A formula we saw wonderfully executed again in Andy Weir's *The Martian*.

In the end, the answer is whatever you want it to be. Some ideas that should be shorts can turn out to be great epics. Some epics should be a lot shorter. The bottom-line relies on the skills of the storyteller. If we're having fun being carried away on the journey, then that's all that matters.

Some of my favorite writers, Stephen King and Robert Heinlein for example, are quite adept at spinning yarns where the getting to is always more fascinating than the destination.

Summing it up

Story length is determined by the following:

- **Number of characters**
- **Scale of conflict**
- **Depth of conflict**
- **The pace of the story**
- **Your writing style**

HOW TO WRITE A BESTSELLING NOVEL ON YOUR IPHONE

I arrive at the restaurant early. I have 30 minutes to kill. I can either waste that time on some social news site reading things I won't remember an hour later, or do something slightly more productive. Usually I opt for the time waster. Sometimes though, I resist temptation and make better use of this time: I use my phone to write a book. Maybe not the whole novel or even half, but I still manage to thumb type entire chapters and sections at a time.

Writing something long form using your thumbs sounds like a form of torture to most people. The truth is, once you get used to it, it's not all that bad. Yesterday I wrote two chapters for an upcoming Jessica Blackwood novel using my iPhone while laying on my couch. I didn't feel like sitting down at my computer. So instead, in the most lazy way possible I still managed to write.

When it's time to write the book itself, I like to be in a distraction-free environment – which can be on an airplane or in the middle of a shopping mall. The distractions I try to avoid the most are the ones I invite on myself.

Sometimes, we can't control those things. My friends often complain that they don't have the time to write because life gets in the way. I call BS on that. Just about anybody can write 1,000 words in an hour. All it takes is 40 hours spread over weeks or months and you have a novel.

The problem is that most people find themselves staring at the screen watching the time fly and the word count not move. Their mistake is that they waited until they had some free time to write to actually think about what to write.

When people imagine themselves writing they conjure the image of the solitary figure hunched over a keyboard hammering away their epic. The truth of the matter, at least for me, probably only 50% of my time spent writing a book is sitting in front of a computer. My novels are outlined over and over on yellow legal pads. Chapters are written and shuffled on index cards. Web pages are saved to Pocket, Wikipedia articles are printed out.

I've written as much as 20,000 words in a day. The trick of it was that I'd solved all the little problems that would have had me staring into space beforehand. That's where planning comes in. That's where your iPhone, Android, iPod or whatever is here to save you.

A novel is a narrative that unifies a bunch of ideas. These ideas can form characters, plots and the details that make your story unique. A really good novel has a lot of ideas. You can come up with more ideas in 5 days than 5 hours. That's what your phone is for. It's probably near you 24-7. Any time inspiration strikes, not necessarily in the form of prose, but the actual molecules that make up a story, make a note.

Ever stare into space thinking up character names? Should a conversation take place in a car or on a side of the road when a taxi got a flat tire? Where did your character go to school? What's the scariest thing that ever happened to them? What kind of house does you antagonist live in?

These are the kind of ideas you can come up with anytime. Just a half dozen pre-planned ideas per chapter will make it all the more interesting.

The problem with a lot of amateur writing is that it feels like they're trying to figure things out too late. Once they have an original thought, the perfect time has passed.

Your phone is the perfect device to capture all the seeds that will flower into the garden that's your book. As I've learned, I can even write my novel on my phone. If that still sounds painful, imagine writing an entire novel, long-form using a quill pen.

We don't get a lot of unbroken, distraction-free time to write. We do have lots of fragmented moments to have singular ideas and thoughts. Use these times appropriately. You won't need to steal away moments to write your novel on your phone if you plan wisely. But if you have to, with clear direction, the time will be much better spent.

Who knows, you might even find you enjoy the time thumb typing away your story. Strangely enough, I do.

So, here's how to use your iPhone to write a novel:

1. Use your note app to write down ideas that will make your novel more interesting and deeper.

2. Make a lot of notes. Have a lot of ideas.

3. Get a mobile app like Byword so you can write anytime you feel like it.

The secret to making a book cover (that mostly doesn't suck) in 10 minutes or less

An ugly cover is all that it takes to keep people away from your book. Although we're not supposed to judge a book by them, let's be honest, if someone can't manage that first impression, we're likely to be skeptical that the inside is any better.

The easiest way to get a good looking cover is to hire a professional. Do a search for "Book Covers" and you'll find hundreds of talented artists who will sell you something pre-made or do a custom cover for you. I've seen some great looking covers for under a hundred books.

Assuming you want to do it yourself and you have a modicum of knowledge using Photoshop, there's a very simple formula I use to create covers. But first, go to a bookstore and roam through the shelves and pay attention to what catches your eye (or take a stroll through Amazon.) Make some notes, then come back here.

Here are my observations:

1. A book cover needs two things, a title and the name of the author. Anything else is eye candy designed to capture your interest.

2. A font choice can be used to communicate part of the story. It can also make your book look tacky.

3. A simple image can be just as powerful as a complex one.

4. Movie poster covers of characters doing things are usually more suited for science fiction and fantasy. Mainstream book covers or less busy.

5. The best covers rarely use people in them. Do a search for "Best book covers" and you'll see what I mean.

Let's take a look at some of the most iconic book covers of all time and break down what's going on:

Jurassic Park
Author: Michael Crichton
Artist: Chip Kidd
A tyrannosaurus skeleton in silhouette. Skeletons are scary. Sharp teeth are scary. Dinosaurs are scary. Combine them all and you have a very scary cover that doesn't need to show the actual animal. It was so iconic, it was the poster for the movie as well.

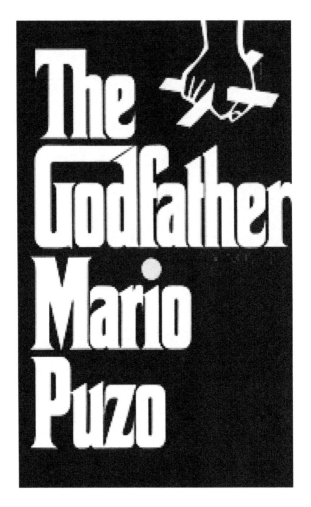

The Godfather
Author: Mario Puzo
Artist: S. Neil Fujita
A puppeteer controlling the letters of "Godfather." This cover was so good they reused it for the film, like *Jurassic Park*'s image.

Psycho
Author: Robert Bloch
Artist: Tony Palladino
All we need are the broken letters of "Psycho" to tell us that there's something very wrong here.

Jaws
Author: Peter Benchley
Artist: Roger Kastel
A girl swimming. A shark about to eat her. That's the essence of tension. For the theatrical poster they used the same concept but made the shark much more realistic with a mouth-full of gnarly teeth.

After looking at these, comes the very simple secret for creating a memorable cover without having to be an amazing artist – but having some appreciation for graphic design.

Most iconic covers combine two elements. A graphic and then something happening to it or a twist.

- The dinosaur skeleton is upright and not extinct.
- Somebody is pulling the strings in "The Godfather."
- The letters in "Psycho" are broken.
- The girl is about to collide with the shark in a not so fun way.

Figure out some iconic aspect to your book that can be communicated in a simple way. Don't try to tell the whole story. The letters in "Psycho" don't tell us the twist. Jaws says nothing about Sheriff Brody. Just pick one important theme that makes your story special.

10 minute covers for totally original, not ripped-off, books
As an experiment, I gave myself 50 minutes to conceive and create five book covers for best-selling novels. I sketched them out on a notepad then started throwing them together.

I didn't do any "drawing" or illustrating. I just grabbed images and figured out interesting ways to juxtapose them in Photoshop.

While the results aren't going to put Chip Kidd out of business anytime soon, I think a couple are better than many self-published books. Not because I have any artistic skill (I don't) but because I stuck to the simple formula.

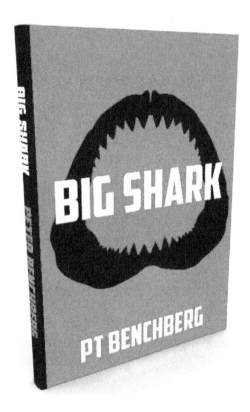

Big Shark = Teeth + Red
I "borrowed" the teeth idea from Jurassic Park and dropped them into this totally original shark eating people fake book.

Wizard Boy = Hat + Stars
The text is handwritten, like on a school notebook. The wizard hat evokes magic and the stars imply destiny.

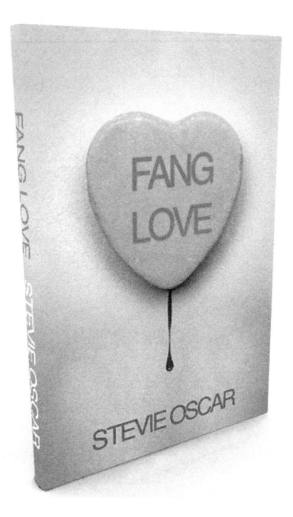

Fang Love = Valentine candy + Blood
There have been a million variations on this idea. Candy is iconic. Blood changes the context of anything.

Whipping Girl = Whips + Bouquet
What could be more romantic? I was running out of time so I just copied the same two riding crops over and over. You get the point. I chose a pink background to make it feminine and curly letters to imply youth.

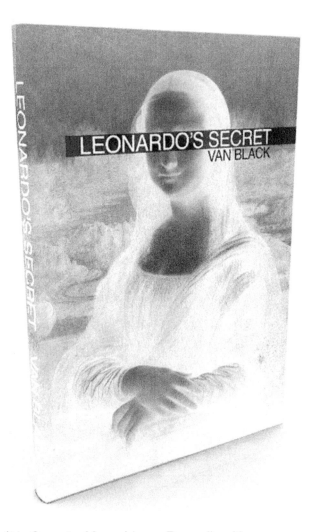

Leonardo's Secret = Mona Lisa + Revealing X-ray
By showing the Mona Lisa in an inverse image, we imply there's something else to be seen. I then put the letters and a black bar over her eyes, implying that it's something she shouldn't see.

For your book cover you should try making a bunch of different simple mockups then spend your time polishing the one you like the most. If I were going to use any of these (which would be weird), I'd go back and make sure all my graphics are cleaned up and everything is proportional.

The secret to the secret is to try a lot of things and throw most of them out.

Why you're staring at a blank screen

Favorite beverage: Check. Comfy clothes: Check. Snacks: Check. Here you are, all set to write your epic and you've already managed to drink and eat all your provisions without moving the cursor. What happened on this trip through imagination? Why did the boat never set sail? How come time is moving forward, but you're standing still?

In my case, I can always blame one reason: I didn't have a map. Sure, I knew I wanted to get to Awesome City. The problem is, that's all I knew. A story isn't what happens. It's how it happens. Did we take a boat? Fly? Was the airport crowded? Did the crew threaten to mutiny before we got aboard?

There are generally two ways to write. One is to sit down and just keep writing until you get to some sort of conclusion. If you're Stephen King and you realized halfway through you've created far too many plot lines; you arbitrarily murder a few in the middle of the book. If you're George RR Martin; well, you just keep writing more books and murder them at your leisure.

The other way, used by lesser mortals like myself, is to have a plan. I sit down with a clear idea of the whole plot and then proceed to show my audience the story. I don't have everything figured out. Far from it. Mainly, I think of all the problems that are going to get in my hero's way. I set them up to fail and then try to help them figure their way out of the mess.

When I'm staring at an empty screen and an empty box of Red Vines, it's because I had an idea of what happened, but no clearly defined conflict. There was nothing pulling me the writer (and ultimately the reader) into the story. All I knew was that Ms. Z needed to find out some crucial information, like the dead man's lungs were filled with salt water. Life is complicated. Storytelling is communicating all the interesting conflicts.

When I'm stuck like this, I have a simple solution: I get up from my keyboard and take a walk. Twenty minutes later, I inevitably have my solution and a renewed enthusiasm.

To avoid this happening, I try to break my outlines into a clear series of conflicts. At each step I need to know what all my character's objectives are and what's stopping them. That makes it crystal clear to me at the start of each chapter what it's about and when it's over.

This isn't for everyone or every style of writing. Some genres thrive on meandering plot lines that never really go anywhere. Romance and period books are often really just about spending time inside that world. Readers pick these books up for escapism, not clever plot twists or information. They just want to be somewhere else while they read them. When you write these kinds of stories it's okay to take all the time you please. Often enough in those stories, once the relationship is consummated, it's all downhill from there anyway.

You can also write and write and then trim it down later. That's the way documentaries are made. Some of the greatest examples of literature came from whittling away much longer stories. This is an equally valid approach. it just takes forever...

Regardless of your approach, if you're staring at that screen and your fingers aren't moving, it's probably because you need to step away and ask yourself *why* things happened instead of just *what*.

- **Take a break and go for a walk**
- **Rewind the story to where it was exciting**
- **What would be an awesome twist that you already laid out the ground work for?**
- **Break down the root of the conflicts**
- **Write anything that comes to your mind**
- **Don't stop!**

ONE WEIRD TRICK TO BOOST YOUR CREATIVITY

Sometimes you need to come up with a lot of ideas. Right now I'm a little obsessed with 2-sentence short stories, so I've been trying to think up as many as I can. I might sit down and have 30 of them, or I might struggle for one before going to bed. You never know when inspiration might strike. A creative mind is always on (unless it's not).

I have a little thing I do to make this easier. I'm a big believer in creating the shortest path from your brain to the real world. A lot of really good ideas never make it into reality. Shortening the path is helpful. This is one way to do that.

I've used this method over and over again. When we were planning the first season of my A&E television show, *Don't Trust Andrew Mayne*, we needed hundreds of ideas for magic effects. Fortunately, I had a database of concepts to start from – an actual, literal database.

Compiling it was pretty painless. If you use Google Drive, you're probably familiar with its ability to create forms. This is an easy way to collect email addresses on a website, fill in questionnaires etc. But forms don't just have to be something you share with the world. I create forms for myself. For the TV magic stuff, I created a form to input an idea whenever I had one. The form let me add fields for the kind of trick and other useful information that made it easy to sort through. All the data goes into a spreadsheet you can sort through at your leisure.

Here's where it gets kind of cool. On your iPhone or Android device you can save that form to your home screen as a web app. I keep a couple on my main screen. Whenever I have an idea, I press the icon and the form pops up. It's pretty easy to just dictate whatever I want if I'm on the go or just too lazy to type. I click submit and BOOM. Idea saved.

You can customize your form however you want. You can create a general idea database, or be more specific. I like to have different spreadsheets for different projects.

Step 1. Go to Google Docs and create a new form

Step 2. Fill in the fields for what information you want to capture

Step 3. Open the form link and save it to your phone home screen as a web app

YOUR WORST IDEA MAY BE YOUR GREATEST

The earliest drafts of *Star Wars** were horrible. Don't believe me? Check out *The Star Wars*, an officially licensed graphic novel of one of the early scripts. It's not just that the character names are all mixed up; the story is barely recognizable to the one we love. It's a weird mix of *Flash Gordon*, *Metropolis* and Isaac Asimov's *Foundation*, in all the bad ways.

It's also genius. Many of the elements that would make *Star Wars* the phenomena it is today are there. We have droids with personalities (R2-D2 even talks, egad!). There's an ancient order of knights trying to bring justice to the universe, a strong-willed princess, Stormtrooper space soldiers that strike both fear and awe, along with space battles and the kind of images only George Lucas could imagine.

Somewhere between Lucas's first imaginings of *Star Wars* as he sat in front of his television watching *Flash Gordon* serials as a kid and that fateful day on May 25th, 1977 when audiences got their first glimpse of the future of space fantasy, something happened.

Yet even after he narrowed the focus of the story to one that was both personal and expansive, there was no guarantee. Early edits of the film and excised scenes are painful to watch. *Star Wars*, even the filmed version, could have been a very bad movie. But it wasn't.

How did this movie evolve from a mess of an outline into one of the most beloved stories of all time?

If one thing is clear from the multitude of biographies and accounts of the making of *Star Wars* (I highly recommend Chris Taylor's *How Star Wars Conquered the Universe*), the movie became a success for two reasons:

1. Lucas stuck with what he loved.
2. Lucas listened to feedback from the right people.

Lucas gave up a lot of his ideas but he kept the ones that stoked his imagination. This is an important thing to remember. If something doesn't work and brings your story down, analyze it. Ask yourself: Why do you love this idea so much?

From Lucas's first film *THX-1138* to *Star Wars* and later the *Clone Wars*, we can see that he was fascinated with faceless space soldiers. A fan of animation, he could look at a trash can with a round head and no face and see a creation that children and adults around the world would fall in love with. The nobility and prowess of the samurai, the excitement of an aerial dogfight, were all elements Lucas wanted to use.

The problem was he didn't have a story. He had a collage of amazing ideas and a not-so-amazing structure. An R2-D2 without a meaningful purpose is just a prop. The same can be said for characters. If they're just there to get your point across or get pushed around on the chessboard of your imagination, they're lifeless puppets with strings that point to a puppeteer.

Star Wars became a *great idea* for a story when Lucas focused on the characters and gave them their own purpose. The true breath of life an author can bestow on a character is their own will. *Star Wars* became a *great script* when he narrowed the focus to a pivotal few days in their life and was able to decide what was absolutely critical to the story and what wasn't. We jump right into the middle of a battle as the Imperial Star Destroyer captures Princess Leia's ship at a make or break moment for the Rebel Alliance. It became a *great production* when Lucas and his team hired amazing talent for both behind and in front of the camera. It became a *great film* when Lucas and his team of editors, including his then wife, Marcia, got rid of the bad parts, used every trick in the book to pull the thing together and created a fast-paced story that gave us enough moments to care for our characters.

The single-most important choice he made was listening to his fellow filmmakers. They told him the story was confusing. They chided the introverted filmmaker for ignoring the people that lived in the universe. His long winded dialog about the nature of the force, political maneuvering and stilted lines were cut to a minimum. Screenwriters Gloria Katz and Willard Huyck helped Lucas shape the characters and give the story a touch of humor. Brian De Palma thought the opening crawl was gibberish and rewrote the succinct three-sentence one we now know. Lucas's editors took the footage and found the story when he was afraid it might not be on film.

Star Wars, was in short, a team effort. But not just any team. These were an incredibly talented group of people that had already won accolades for their own work and would go to do outstanding non-*Star Wars* films.

If you're sitting there thinking to yourself that's just swell, but you don't have any Academy Award winners you can call up on speed dial, that's not the point. To make what you're doing better, you can start by getting feedback from someone who knows a little more than you. If I want to make my books more scientifically accurate, I ask a scientist. If I want to give the characters more depth, I talk to someone who knows character-driven stories. No one person may have the all the answers. Nobody did on *Star Wars*. But a lot of smart people around Lucas were able to help him do everything from make the story more streamlined to figuring out what a Millennium Falcon should look like.

Break your work into a bunch of smaller questions. Do you care about these characters? Do you understand their objective? Is this universe real? Look around you for people that can tell you. Keep casting a wider net for talent.

Lucas got to the point he could work with the greatest talent in the world because he started by making the best use of the talent available to him as a student.

Once he had that talent around him, he stuck to what he loved, even when they didn't get it. This is what makes George Lucas one of the most imaginative storytellers ever. Where the people around him could help shape his vision and bring clarity, it was up to Lucas to provide the raw material for them to work with and to inspire the other creators he collaborated with.

*A note to all the pedantic nerds out there. I called it *Star Wars* and not *Episode IV* or *A New Hope* because that's what the damn movie was called when it was originally released. The *New Hope* and *Episode IV* revisionist nonsense didn't start until Lucas re-released the film just prior to *The Empire Strikes Back*. He changed the title and millions of nerds went along with it, opening the door to all of the *Special Editions* and revisions to come. You have only yourselves to blame.

You suck at taking criticism

Taking criticism, corrections, suggestions, input or any other kind of feedback that isn't complete praise, is hard. For some of us, it's really, really painful. Even the most objective, well-intentioned observation can set us off.

The conventional advice is to either ignore it or get a thicker skin. I suggest a third option: Understand it.

I was just at a conference and listened to a table full of writers explain that they don't read their Amazon reviews. This was crazy to me. Although I don't hang on every review and I don't take every five-star blurb as a justification for my existence or every negative one as proof that the reviewer is the most awful person in the world. To be honest, I pay less attention to my reviews than my friends or family does, but I'm aware of them.

I like to think like a scientist. One or two people who hate something I did is just statistical noise. A few more than that and it's worth understanding. Five star praise is wonderful, but well-thought explanations as to why someone gave you a three or four is priceless information. (But let me really make it clear, people who give me five star reviews are perfect beings of light who have my undying love.)

I have a very small circle of people who could potentially give me the kind of criticism that would create self-doubt. They never have. They've given me lots and lots of notes. They've told me which ideas are great, which are not so good. They've poked holes in my brilliant theories. They've pointed out my remedial blunders. Never once has any of them made me second-guess my ability as a storyteller.

If you're going to flourish as a creative, you have to understand criticism. A classic mistake is to avoid anything except praise and to shut out the people that may actually know a thing or two that could make you better at what you're trying to do.

We all want to be the prodigy; perfect from the start. This is not only impossible, it's boring. People on a journey are far more interesting.

I once took a comedy class and heard an interesting story about a young comic the teacher knew. According to the instructor, this kid was an awful stand-up. Despite that, he constantly begged to get booked in shows and even offered to drive the headliners around for a ten minute spot. The booker relented and would occasionally throw him gigs even though the kid would bomb.

A bad Amazon review or YouTube comment is nothing like having someone tell you that you suck while you're on stage. You can practice with your band in a garage and have a reasonable idea how you'll do on your first gig. As a magician I get to rely on proven methods. The only way to get good at stand-up is by putting yourself through the most painful process in show business.

Audiences and other comics constantly told this comic he sucked, but he kept at it.

When he drove the headliners to shows he'd barrage them with questions and ask for advice. He kept performing and sucking. But he was persistent. Then one day, the booker couldn't determine when, the young comic was getting laughs instead of boos. The advice had sunk in and the stage time had started showing its effect. People began thinking he was hilarious. His comedy kept improving and he didn't have to beg for shows. This comic (Chris Rock by the way) went on to star on SNL, have a series of HBO specials and become an Emmy and Grammy winner.

Like almost all comics, Chris Rock didn't start out being funny on stage. He had to earn that. He had to persist. He didn't ignore the criticism, he learned to understand it. He sought out the advice of people who understood comedy and he kept improving.

For writers taking the traditional route, the path is filled with piles of rejection letters with feedback from professional editors. Fun fact: *Harry Potter* was turned down 40 times!

For self-published writers, our path is online reviews written by amateurs and indifference. Be careful to reading too much into either, but ignore them at your own peril.

THE CURSE OF A CREATIVE MIND

I'm going to tell you how to figure out which of your ideas is the best one. But before we get started, I'm going to do a little psychoanalysis on you and tell you about your problems.

Have a seat on my couch. Please help yourself to some Red Vines. Ready?

Tell me if this sounds familiar:

You have a head full of ideas and you're constantly thinking up new projects – yet never seem to get anything done?

Why is it some nights you burst awake with an idea and a million gigawatts of enthusiasm, but a week later it's the most boring thing you can imagine?

The answer is simple: You're creative.

That doesn't just mean you're expressive or that you have a clever way of looking at things. It also mean you're compulsively seeking new connections and patterns. You're an idea junky. You love the little fix your brain gives you every time you think up something new.

This is a great way to be. But it also has its drawbacks. We're creative because we want the world to be a little different. We want our own path. We hate the dull, boring parts of life.

The problem with getting anything done is that some of the things we have to do to get us there aren't the cool parts. Writing a book and need to create backstory when you want to jump right into the plot? Want to make a movie but there's a lack of script in the way? Want to bring life to a roles as an actor but the audition process is wearing you down?

These are the most critical moments you face. Successful people find a way through. Unsuccessful people find something else shiny and new.

99% of my life has been spent chasing projects I gave up when I came up with that newer, more awesome idea. Was it really a better idea? Probably not. It only seemed more awesome because at the starting line I can't see all the hurdles or truly understand what that lung-burning exhaustion is going to feel like when the finish line is still out of sight.

For years my daily conversation with my buddy Justin Robert Young, was my new, awesome, world-changing idea. We'd drive to Taco Bell, Arby's or Costco on sample Fridays and I'd explain my latest scheme. For the most part, I'm sure they were all quite clever. In practical terms, they were useless. Because no matter how excited I was as I explained my concept over roast beef and curly fries, it was a safe bet that in 24 hours I'd have moved on to something else. Does this sound familiar?

The problem with being creative is you can come up with a million reasons to give up on something. You convince yourself you're not quitting, you're just going in a "better" direction. You're fooling yourself. You want to do the new thing because you realized the old thing is hard.

Great things come from getting through the hard parts. And the best solution isn't to just "power through" them. The smart solution is to apply your creativity in a new direction on the same problem.

Does your story feel boring halfway into it? What can you change earlier on to make it more exciting? Is there a way to make your character more deeper and interesting than you realized? Trying to finish a script but not making much progress? Pick ten great movies and steal one thing from each one to add into your film. Making a weekly podcast and getting bored? Change the topic to your new passion.

My greatest successes have always come from the ideas I stuck to, even when I had a million better ones. Next time you're on the verge of changing directions, don't do it. Finish it. A completed mediocre idea is infinitely better than an unfinished stroke of genius. Now get off my couch. We have work to do.

So, to answer the question we started at the beginning:

Your best idea is the one you're working on right now.

How to Make Sure Your Self-Published Book Doesn't Look Self-Published

Services like CreateSpace make it super-simple to produce printed copies of your book. They also make it real easy to make mistakes if you don't know what you're doing. Most self-published books would look much better if their creators took the time to look at a "real" book and notice what to do and what not to.

1. Don't use "by" on the cover.

2. Use proper paragraph formatting (don't space paragraphs in fiction). Don't use crazy big first paragraph indents!

3. Use the right font size. If you have more than 350 words per page, you might have a problem.

4. Fonts matter. Don't go crazy with different styles.

5. Less is more when it comes to cover design. You can buy some great cover art for cheap. If you're a writer, you might not be a designer – keep that in mind.

6. Front matter matters. This is where your copyright page and other meta data goes.

7. Watch your pagination. Real books don't start numbering pages until the first or second page of the story.

8. Watch your headers. Avoid using headers on the start of a new chapter. (It's a style thing.)

9. Don't make your back cover text too small/big.

10. Your back cover shouldn't read like a desperate resume.

Finally! Go look at some "real" books. Seriously! Pay attention to the design (not just the cover) and the choices that were made.

My 5 Favorite Writing Tools

1. Noise-canceling headphones
I use a pair of Bose's QuietComfort in-ear active noise-cancelling headphones whenever I want to tune out the world. They're not cheap (around $300), but they're an important part of my writing process. They make external noises much quieter and keep me very focused. They're great on an airplane and wonderful just sitting in a room by myself.

2. iPhone camera
I use my phone camera to take pictures of police stations, constructions sites, restaurants, hospitals and just about any other location I might want to use in a story. Instead of scratching my head trying to make stuff up, I just flip through my photo album and look at what I'm writing about.

3. Laser printer
Laser printers are now under $100 and allow you to print super cheaply compared to inkjet from Amazon for $99). I highly recommend you get one. Research shows that we process information differently than when it's on a screen versus in a physical piece of media.

With a laser printer and the liberating freedom of printing anything you feel like without having to pay a king's ransom in printer ink, comes these benefits:

- You'll notice all kinds of typos when you have it on a printed piece of paper.
- You can print out physical copies to give to your friends to review.
- Printing your pages after a chapter is finished is very satisfying.

4. Composition notebooks
I've tried everything from legal pads to special software and have settled on using old school composition notebooks for putting my thoughts together and mapping out my books. The first thing I do when I sit down to write in the morning is pull up my notes and sketch out a chapter outline. When I go to lunch, I take the notebook for my current book with me and write down whatever comes to mind. Portable, cheap and battery free, they're a great way to keep track of your book.

5. My Kindle(s)
Before I upload an ebook to Amazon, I make sure it looks good on a Kindle PaperWhite, Kindle HD, my iPhone and my iPad. You want to make sure it'll look good on whatever screen people choose to read it on. Don't have a Kindle? You can buy one here starting at $50.

HOW I NAMED THIS BOOK

Titles can be really hard. Take this book for example: I thought I had a really catchy title, *How to Write a Book in 24 Hours*, then I found over a dozen other books on Amazon with the same name. If you want to stand out, you should probably choose something a little more original.

I decided to change it up a little and thought *How to Write a Novella in 24 Hours* sounded almost as good. But would people know what a novella was? So then I tried *How to Write a Fiction Book in 24 Hours*. Was that too wordy? Decisions, decisions.

I sent instant messages to five friends and received two for either and one undecided. Thanks guys.

I finally decided to just ask people on Twitter what they thought. I created a form on Google Docs and tweeted out a link. Within minutes I had a flood of responses to give me an idea which direction I should go in.

30% more people liked *How to Write a Novella in 24 Hours*. Not exactly a landslide, but enough for me think that wouldn't be the worst decision in the world. While there's no guarantee that all those people would buy the book (actually, they won't – because I'm giving them free copies) it's a tiny ray of light in a cloud of confusion.

Crowdsourcing a title is nothing new. If I wanted to be even more enterprising, I'd take out Google Ads and see which one people clicked on. However, I'm wary of SEO'ing something until you forget why you wanted to do it in the first place.

Another option is to let someone else write it for you. I promise you that 99% of these ideas will be bad and the people with the worst ones will be the most argumentative about why it's brilliant.

To increase the pool of suggestions to people that haven't read your book, provide them with a succinct description of the book and anything else that might be relevant (character names, etc.)

Beyond marketing, you want a title that feels right to you and your audience. I think I've had a mostly good track record with titles because I look for ones that sound familiar but have never actually been in mass media.

For my first novel, *Public Enemy Zero*, I decided to combine the wanted man theme of being a public enemy with the medical term of a "patient zero" – two themes that are critical to the book. The end result was catchy and sold a lot of books.

I did the same with *Angel Killer*. It was an evocative title about the villain. Although it confused the very religious, it sold a lot of books – making me the 5th best-selling author in the UK the year it came out (even though I'm an American.)

For my hard-science time traveller story, I chose *The Chronological Man.* This did a pretty good job of pulling in people who love that genre.

While I personally like some of my other titles, *The Grendel's Shadow*, *Knight School* and *Hollywood Pharaohs*, I don't think they have as much grab as the first three. I truly regret calling the second Chronological Man book "The Martian Emperor," because I think people thought it would be about an actual Martian – and not a giant conspiracy (I still love the book.) *Hollywood Pharaohs* was one of the highest rated mysteries on Amazon the summer it came out, but I don't think the title served it as well as it could. And I still can't spell "pharaohs" exactly right every time.

The right amount of words
A title can be just one word (excluding "the"):

Jaws
Godfather
Dune
Psycho
Twilight
1984
Firm
Hobbit
Exorcist
Lolita
Misery

Or it can be a lot of words that would never appear together randomly:

Harry Potter and the Philosopher's Stone
Gone with the Wind
50 Shades of Grey
Charlie and the Chocolate Factory
The Hitchhiker's Guide to the Galaxy
The Lion, the Witch and the Wardrobe
The Catcher in the Rye
A Tale Of Two Cities

There's no right or wrong answer if a title should be long or short. Harry Potter had a US title, *Harry Potter and the Sorcerer's Stone* and a UK title, *Harry Potter and the Philosopher's Stone* – although it should be pointed out that the US version by Scholastic was the one that sold gazillions of copies and really launched the phenomena.

Some titles can seem plain weird, but work out just fine, like *The Hunger Games*. I can imagine a lot of people saying that's a terrible title (myself included), only to be proven wrong.

I think the most important factor is a title that people who read your book will remember and understand the context.

- **Check to see if your title has already been used (you can call it anything you want, but you want to be unique.)**
- **Ask your friends what they think**
- **Ask your followers on social media**

Ask yourself these questions:

If it's a powerful one-word title, is it relevant?
Lots of books and films have one-word titles that are a little too vague. You want to make sure yours is on point.

Does the title evoke interest?
The book *Goodbye Piccadilly, Farewell Leicester Square* was a bit whimsical for a story about a serial killer. Alfred Hitchcock used the title *Frenzy* when he adapted it for film.

Is it extremely memorable?
Gone with the Wind is a great expression. James Patterson's Alex Cross series brilliantly used nursery rhymes for titles like *Kiss the Girls*, *Pop Goes the Weasel* and *Along Came a Spider*, etc. R.L. Stine would choose the title (*Little Shop of Hamsters*) and then write the book!

AUTHOR THANKS

I hope you found something useful here. If so, I'd love it if you wrote a blurb on Amazon or Goodreads. I can't tell you how much this means to me when someone takes the time to do that.

If you'd like to keep up to date with what I'm up to and my future projects, please sign up for me email list at AndrewMayne.com.

You can follow me online at:
Twitter.com/AndrewMayne
Facebook.com/AndrewMayne

I also have lots of videos about writing and other topics at: YouTube.com/AndrewMayne and I do a weekly podcast on creativity that can be found at WeirdThings.com.

Thank you for reading this!

Best,

Andrew Mayne
@AndrewMayne

100 No (or low) Cost Ways to Promote Your Ebook

This list is meant to get you thinking. I'm not promising that they're all good ideas for you or immediately practical. But quite a few have helped me out.

1. Tweet out the book link when you first release it.

2. Tweet out each time you put it on a new platform.

3. Create a serialized podcast.

4. Personally email +20 friends and ask them to email 10 of their friends. Write the actual email you want them to forward.

5. Announce the book on Facebook.

6. Announce the book on Google+.

7. Create an audiobook versions using Audible's ACX program.

8. Make a short trailer for Vine or Instagram.

9. Ask a group of friends to retweet a link to the book on a specific day.

10. Ask friends via personal email to write reviews for the book.

11. Ask anyone who likes the book on Twitter to write a review for the book.

12. Send an email with positive reviews to your mailing list.

13. Make a mailing list of close friends.

14. Hold a contest for people to make a blurb just on the cover and tweet it out.

15. Call 10 people on your phone and ask them to help promote.

16. Hold a Google Hangout to talk about the book.

17. Create a YouTube video of you talking about the book.

18. Change all your avatars to the book.

19. Promote the book in your signature line.

20. Write a Google+ post on why you wrote the book.

21. Tweet out the post.

22. Email the post.

23. Tweet really good reviews with a thank you.

24. Ask a fan to make a video review for Amazon.

25. Write about something you learned writing the book and submit it to a site like Reddit.

26. Write about something technical/scientific you learned and submit it to Hacker News.

27. Tweet and post small facts about the research for your book.

28. Tweet and post Easter eggs.

29. Tweet and post a list of books that influenced your book.

30. Tweet and post a list of movies that influenced your book.

31. Send out a press release to free services.

32. Ask to be a guest on book related podcasts.

33. Ask to be a guest on topic related podcasts.

34. Put your best reviews in your description.

35. Ask people on Facebook, Twitter and Google+ for promotion ideas.

36. Post several different synopsis and ask people which one they like better.

37. Do the same with alternate covers.

38. Post why you chose the cover you used.

39. Post covers that inspired you.

40. Create an audio trailer for your book and link to it.

41. Create a Twitter feed for one of your characters.

42. Ask people who've read your book who they would cast in a movie then retweet and post their answers.

43. Record a scene from your book as a radio play.

44. Create a Flickr and Instagram feed of photos of locations that inspired you.

45. Make an annotated map of locations.

46. Cross-promote it with other ebooks.

47. Hold a contest for people to do their own 'movie voice' narration for the trailer.

48. Create a list of blogs that review ebooks and send them free copies.

49. Give away a limited number of copies of your ebook.

50. Send printed books to super fans.

51. Use printed versions as prizes.

52. Write guest posts on other blogs.

53. Change categories if it's not ranking on a top 100 list.

54. Use rankings in your description.

55. Create a post where you interview one of your characters.

56. Take a look at the descriptions of the ten best-selling books in your category. Rewrite your description from what you learned.

57. Post the first half of your book for free.

58. Hold an author reading on Google Hangout.

59. Write a guest post unrelated to your book, but mention it in your byline.

60. Write and give away a short story that takes place in your book's universe.

61. Release the prologue as a YouTube video.

62. Remind people there's a free Kindle app for every major platform and provide a link to your book.

63. Do a charity promotion where all proceeds from sales help a cause.

64. Hire someone on Fiverr to help promote your book. (But don't pay for reviews! This is more trouble than it's worth.)

65. Do a cross interview with another author looking to promote their book.

66. Offer to Skype with any fan that has questions.

67. Make an Animoto trailer for your book using free images.

68. Create a Prezi typography presentation of your book (create a video for YouTube).

69. Get your friends to stage Instagram photos of scenes from the book.

70. Exchange Social Media accounts with another author for a day.

71. Use puppets to act out a scene from the book.

72. Send physical copies of the book to people in exotic locations.

73. Ask podcasts if you can put the audio version at the end of their show in a serialized form.

74. Hide a physical copy of your book somewhere and tweet out clues.

75. Have your friends all post photos reading the book.

76. Make paper book jackets that can slip over a Kindle or iPad.

77. Virtually sign ebooks by taking a photo of you next to a white board with your fan's names.

78. Virtually take photos with fans by holding up an iPad with their photo.

79. Hold a contest for people to write the best 140 character or less blurb for the book.

80. Ask fans to tweet photos of the best temporary tattoo relating to the book.

81. Create a new cover for the book.

82. Make a print version (via CreateSpace) and announce it for sale.

83. Include chapters from this book at the end of another one.

84. Make your ebook part of a bundle (like Humble Bundle.)

85. Make your book free for a day.

86. Include your book in Amazon's KDP select program.

87. Create a Spritz (fast moving text) of the first chapter.

88. Hype up the sequel and remind people to get the first version.

89. Offer the book for free to anyone who retweets a sales link.

90. Update your website with new images and info, then tweet about it.

91. Offer free books to anybody who will follow you on Twitter.

92. Announce the book will be free for a day if you get a specific number of retweets or forwards (then make it free anyway.)

93. Make a crossword based on the book.

94. Create t-shirts for the book using catchphrases.

95. Animate a scene using PhotoPuppet for iOS.

96. Put together a music playlist for your book.

97. Compile a list of your fan's favorite things about the book.

98. Post the first sentence of the book on Twitter. Have a "read more" that goes to a larger post with the first chapter. Have another "read more" that then takes them to the Amazon page to buy the book.

99. Post the first chapter on Facebook

100. Create a GIF trailer for the book.

Also by Andrew Mayne

Public Enemy Zero
The Grendel's Shadow
Hollywood Pharaohs
Knight School

Jessica Blackwood:
Angel Killer
Name of the Devil

The Chronological Man:
Monster in the Mist
The Martian Emperor

ANGEL
KILLER

A JESSICA BLACKWOOD NOVEL

ANDREW
MAYNE

NAME OF THE DEVIL

A JESSICA BLACKWOOD NOVEL

ANDREW

AUTHOR OF *ANGEL KILLER*

MAYNE

ANDREW MAYNE

PUBLIC ENEMY ZERO

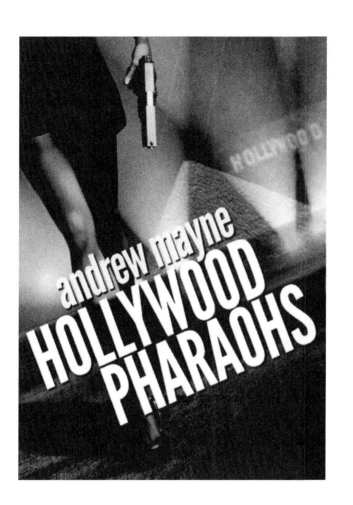

THE **CHRONOLOGICAL MAN**
{A Tale of Scientific Adventure by Andrew Mayne}
The Monster in the Mist

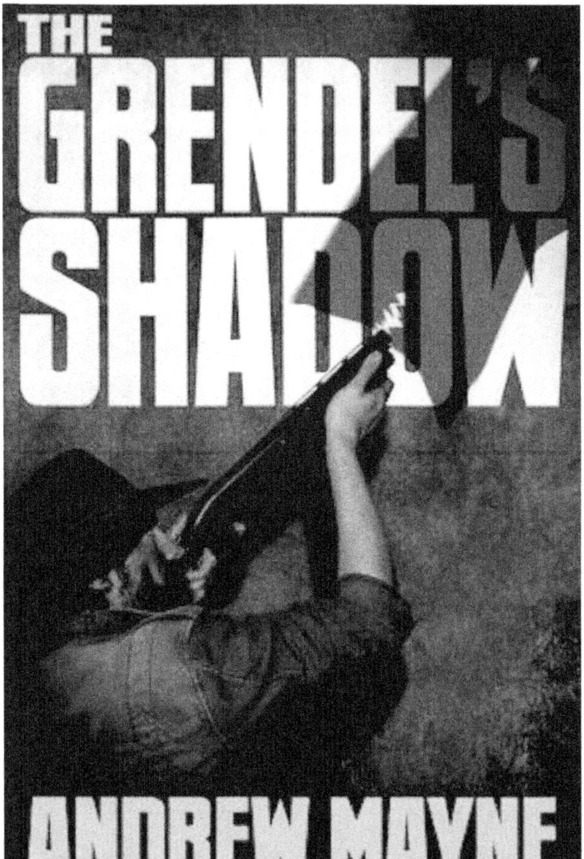
THE
GRENDEL'S
SHADOW
ANDREW MAYNE

KNIGHT
SCHOOL

ANDREW MAYNE

About the Author

Andrew Mayne, star of A&E's Don't Trust Andrew Mayne, is a magician and novelist ranked the fifth best-selling independent author of the year by Amazon UK. He started his first world tour as an illusionist when he was a teenager and went on to work behind the scenes for Penn & Teller, David Blaine and David Copperfield. He's also the host of the WeirdThings.com podcast. AndrewMayne.com

Did I forget to mention I have an email list at AndrewMayne.com?

Printed in Great Britain
by Amazon

34208595R00056